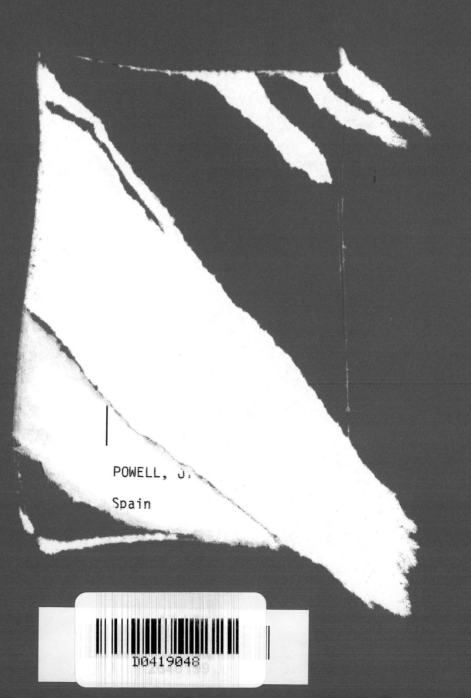

SPAIN

Jillian Powell

FRANKLIN WATTS

LONDON • SYDNEY

First published in 2006 by Franklin Watts
338 Euston Road
London NW1 3BH

Franklin Watts Australia
Level 17/207 Kent Street
Sydney, NSW 2000

ISBN: 978 0 7496 6475 6
Dewey classification: 914.6

Series editor: Sarah Peutrill
Art director: Jonathan Hair
Design: Storeybooks Ltd
Cover design: Peter Scoulding
Picture research: Diana Morris

Picture credits: Jose Aitzelai/AGE: 25b. Paco
Ayala/AGE: 12, 22. Bernd Ducke/A1 Pix: front cover
main, 7, 9, 14, 26b. Macduff Everton/Image
Works/Topfoto: 21tl. Eye Ubiquitous/Hutchison: 4, 19.
Paco Gómez García/AGE: 13. Gunter Gräfenhain/A1
Pix: 18. HAGA/A1 Pix: 10tr, 24. Kneer/A1 Pix: front
cover inset, 1, 11. Koserowsky/A1 Pix: 15b. Javier
Larrea/AGE: 15t, 17b. Petra Loewen/A1 Pix: 21cr.
Alberto Paredes/AGE: 17t, 23. Prosport/Topfoto: 25t.
Jordi Puig/AGE: 10bl. José Fuste Raga/zefa/Corbis: 27.
David Samuel Robbins/Corbis: 20. P. Siegenthaler/A1
Pix: 6, 8, 16. Superstock: 26t.

A CIP catalogue record for this book is available from
the British Library.

Printed in China

Franklin Watts is a division of Hachette Children's
Books, an Hachette Livre UK company.

Contents

Where is Spain?

Spain is in south-western Europe.

Spain

Spain is the second largest country (after France) in western Europe.

Madrid is the capital city of Spain. It has grand squares, avenues, buildings and parks, and a world-famous art gallery called the Prado.

The Plaza Major (main square) in Madrid has a statue of King Philip III.

Use this map to find the places mentioned in this book.

Did you know?

Madrid is the highest capital city in Europe.

Spain has borders with four other European countries and a coastline along the Bay of Biscay, the Atlantic Ocean and the Mediterranean Sea. The Balearic Islands and the Canary Islands, off the coast of West Africa, are part of Spain.

The landscape

Spain has a very varied landscape.

There are huge areas of flat farmland.
In the middle of the country is a
high plateau called the Meseta.

Meseta means 'table'
because the land here
is mostly flat.

In the hot, dry south there is even an area of semi-desert.

Jaén in Andalucia, with the Sierra Nevada mountains behind.

Spain also has high mountain ranges including the Pyrénées and the Cantabrian mountains in the north, and the Sierra Nevada in the south.

Weather and seasons

On the Meseta, it can be very hot and dry in summer, and freezing cold in winter.

Around the Mediterranean Sea, in the south and on the Balearic Islands, there is a Mediterranean climate – hot sunny summers and mild winters.

Did you know?

Parts of Spain have sunshine for 300 of the 365 days in a year!

The hot sunny summers and mild winters of Spain's Costa del Sol make it popular with tourists all year round.

Snow sports like skiing are popular in the Sierra Nevada.

Northern Spain and the mountain areas have more rain and a cooler climate. In winter, there is heavy snow in the Pyrénées and the Sierra Nevada.

Did you know?

Sierra Nevada means snowy mountains in Spanish.

Spanish people

The Spanish people are proud of their culture. They have practised some traditions, like bull-fighting and Flamenco song and dance, for hundreds of years.

Did you know?

The caves at Altamira in northern Spain have paintings inside them that were painted over 14,000 years ago.

Dancers in folk costume celebrate the festival of Saint Joseph in Valencia.

There are many different religions in Spain. Most Spanish people are Roman Catholic, but there are also Protestants, Muslims and Jews.

A Roman Catholic woman lights a candle in the cathedral in Barcelona.

Spanish people shopping at a market in Mallorca for fresh local foods.

Spain is divided into different regions, which each have their own traditions, folk costume and styles of cooking. Some regions, such as Catalonia and the Basque region, have their own flags and languages, too.

Spanish children

Most Spanish children start school when they are two or three years old, and stay until they are 16. They then start training for work, or study longer so they can go on to college or university.

The school day starts at 8.30 or 9 am and goes on until 5 pm. There is a long lunch break at midday, which is the hottest time of the day.

Did you know?

Spanish children usually have two surnames, from their mother's and their father's name.

Spanish children at work in their school library.

Children enjoy a game of football in the town of Ávila.

After school, children enjoy playing sports or watching television.

In Spain, family life is very important. Big families often get together, and children join adults for eating out, even late into the evening. Evenings are also a time for walking, window shopping and meeting friends.

Country

Fewer than a quarter of Spanish people live in the country. Many younger people have moved away to find work in the towns and cities.

In the country, most people make a living from the land or keeping animals. Cattle are kept mainly in the north, and sheep and goats in the south and on the Balearic Islands.

A shepherd in central Spain leads his flock of sheep.

Wheat, barley and sunflowers are the main crops grown in Spain. In the hot, dry south, olives, almonds, oranges and lemons are also grown.

The dry summer climate in Spain helps crops like wheat to ripen.

Did you know?

Spain is one of the least crowded countries in Europe.

A farmhouse surrounded by almond trees on the island of Mallorca.

City

Most people in Spain live in towns or cities, often in the suburbs, travelling into the centre to work. The largest cities are the capital, Madrid, and Barcelona, which is in the region of Catalonia.

The Plaza Mayor and cathedral of Segovia.

Spanish towns and cities are mostly built around a main square called *plaza mayor*.

Did you know?

Spanish plazas can be round, oval or rectangular as well as square.

The cities are the richest and busiest places in Spain, with many tourists visiting cities such as Seville as well as the coastal and island resorts. Public transport includes buses, trains and electric trams.

An electric tram in the city of Bilbao.

Spanish homes

In the south, many Spanish homes are built from clay or stone with small windows, shutters and whitewashed walls to keep them cool. The older houses are built on narrow streets.

Typical whitewashed houses in Córdoba in Andalucia.

Inside, homes often have tiles on the walls and floors, which also helps to keep them cool.

Some of these flats in Seville have balconies with glass walls.

In towns and cities, most people live in blocks of flats in the centre or in the suburbs. Some blocks have shops on the ground floor.

Each flat has a balcony – an outside space for growing plants in pots or drying washing.

Did you know?

In southern Spain, some people live in cave homes, built into rocky hill-sides.

Food

Food is an important part of family life for the Spanish.

As well as supermarkets and small shops like bakeries and groceries, Spanish towns and cities have markets where people can buy fresh fish, meat, fruit and vegetables. Many regions have their own foods and styles of cooking.

Markets offer many types of fresh food, and often clothes and household goods as well.

Many Spanish restaurants and cafés have tables for eating outside.

Paella is a popular Spanish dish containing rice, shellfish, meat, peppers and olives.

Spanish people enjoy sitting down for a big midday meal together, or going out in the evening to eat at restaurants or café bars. Most bars serve tapas, which are small plates of many different snack foods like sausages, fish or potatoes.

Did you know?

The word *paella* means pan; in Spain, people usually cook, and share, this meal in a large pan.

At work

Many city people work in offices.

Spanish people work in shops, offices, hotels, banks, schools, factories, farming and fishing. Madrid is the centre for offices and banks. Barcelona and the Basque country are important industrial centres.

Did you know?

Spain has the biggest fishing fleet in the European Union.

In cities and coastal towns many people work in the tourist industry. Over 50 million tourists visit Spain every year. They also buy Spanish crafts like pottery, leather, jewellery and rugs.

⊚ Tourism provides jobs in hotels, restaurants, cafés and bars. This waiter is serving tapas.

Spanish factories make cars, machine tools, plastics and textiles. There are also factories that process chemicals or food, wines and sherries.

Having fun

There are many colourful fiestas, or festivals, in Spain. Some celebrate Roman Catholic saints or religious days, others the harvest or local foods. There are often noisy street parades and firework displays and people celebrate with dancing, singing and eating.

Did you know?

The region of Valencia has a tomato-throwing festival.

Flamenco dancers at the April fair in Seville, which attracts visitors from all over the world.

Teams like Réal Madrid make Spain a leading football nation.

Football, tennis, golf and cycling are all popular sports in Spain. Some sports have been practised in Spain for hundreds of years. They include the ball game of *Pelota*, which is played on a walled court by four players, and the spectator sport of bull-fighting.

Millions of people play the Spanish lotteries. The most famous is *El Gardo*, which means 'the fat one'.

Spain: the facts

Spain is a monarchy. The king is the head of state, and a president leads the government. The country is divided into 17 regions, which each has its own elected government.

Spain is a member of the European Union. The Spanish use the European currency, the euro.

The euro (left) replaced the old Spanish currency of pesetas (right) in 2002.

The Spanish flag has bands of yellow and red and bears the national coat of arms, which shows the union of four old kingdoms.

Barcelona is the second biggest city in Spain. Around 1.5 million people live there.

Over 44 million people live in Spain today; more than three million live in the capital city Madrid.

Did you know?

There are more than 10,000 castles in Spain.

Glossary

Balearic Islands a group of islands in the Mediterranean Sea, including Mallorca, Minorca and Ibiza.

Bull-fighting a spectator sport popular in Spain, Portugal and parts of South America in which a trained bull-fighter (matador) fights a bull.

Canary Islands a group of seven islands in the Atlantic Ocean, off the northwestern coast of Africa. Although quite far from the mainland, the islands belong to Spain.

Coat of arms the symbols of a family or country.

Culture the ideas, beliefs and art of a people or nation.

Currency the money used by a country or group of countries.

European Union a group of European countries that have joined together to share trade, some laws, and, if they choose to, a single currency (the Euro).

Fiesta a festival.

Flamenco a type of music using song, foot stamping and the guitar, often with dancing.

Head of state the main representative of a country; sometimes the leader of the government.

Meseta the high flat land in the middle of Spain.

Monarchy a country that has a king or queen.

Plateau an area of high, flat land.

President the leader of a government in Spain. In some countries a Prime Minister is the leader.

Roman Catholic a member of the Christian faith who follows Roman Catholic beliefs.

Suburbs the area outside a town or city, where people mostly live rather than work.

Traditions ways and beliefs that have been passed down through generations.

Find out more

About Spain:
www.oxfam.org.uk/coolplanet/ ontheline/explore/journey/spain
A virtual journey of Spain, including sections on food, sport, music and dance.

www.bbc.co.uk/nature/reallywild /features/holiday_guide/spain
Guide to wildlife for children travelling to Spain, with information on birds and animals to look out for.

Learning Spanish:
bbc.co.uk/schools/primary spanish
The BBC schools website for learning Spanish, including simple phrases and help in mastering Spanish letter sounds.

www.apples4theteacher.com/ foreignlang.html/spanish
Interactive games to help teach Spanish numbers, alphabet sounds and facial features.

Note to parents and teachers: Every effort has been made by the Publishers to ensure that these websites are suitable for children, that they are of the highest educational value, and that they contain no inappropriate or offensive material. However, because of the nature of the Internet, it is impossible to guarantee that the contents of these sites will not be altered. We strongly advise that Internet access is supervised by a responsible adult.

Some Spanish words

Spanish word	English word	Say ...
adiós	goodbye	uh-dee-os
de nada	you're welcome	day na-duh
hola	hello	oh-luh
gracias	thank you	gra-si-as
qué tal?	how are you?	kay tal?
lo siento	I'm sorry	lah see-en-toh
me llamo	my name is	may yuh-moh
no	no	no
perdón	excuse me	per-don
por favor	please	por fuh-vor
si	yes	see

My map of Spain

Trace this map and use the map on page 5 to write the names of all the towns.

Index